When Grandma visited Alaska she ...

came to see the many wonderful things
this state has to offer.
This is the story
of her adventurous journey.

Acknowledgements:
We are grateful to the following for repeatedly assisting us with our book projects:
Bob & Pam Gilbertson, Ingo Richter, Lynne Beykirch, Pam "the Grammar Cop" Patterson,
Scott & Kasey Goss, Cindy & Wray Kinard, Dean Philips, and our editor, Linda Thurston.

To our parents and grandparents
who never had the opportunity to visit this great land of Alaska.

Designed, produced, published, and distributed in Alaska by:
  Bernd and Susan Richter
  Saddle Pal Creations, Inc., P.O. Box 872127, Wasilla, AK 99687, USA

**More children's books by Bernd and Susan Richter available
from Saddle Pal Creations, Inc.:**

* *I See You Through My Heart*
* *Grandma and Grandpa Cruise Alaska's Inside Passage*
* *Grandma and Grandpa Visit Denali National Park*
* *Uncover Alaska's Wonders (a lift-the-flap book)*
* *Alaska Animals - Where Do They Go at 40 Below?*
* *Touch and Feel Alaska's Animals (board book)*
* *The Twelve Days of Christmas in Alaska*
* *The Little Bear Who Didn't Want to Hibernate*
* *Traveling Alaska*
* *Goodnight Alaska - Goodnight Little Bear (board book)*
* *Peek-A-Boo Alaska (lift-the-flap board book)*
* *How Animal Moms Love Their Babies (board book)*
* *When Grandma and Grandpa cruised through AK (board book)*

* *How Alaska Got Its Flag (with flag song CD)*
* *Discover Alaska's Denali Park*
* *Do Alaskans Live in Igloos?*
* *Cruising Alaska's Inside Passage*
* *Listen to Alaska's Animals (sound book)*
* *She's My Mommy Too!*
* *There Was A Little Porcupine*
* *Alaskan Toys for Girls and Boys*
* *My Alaska Animals - Can You Name Them?*
* *A Bus Ride Into Denali (board book)*
* *There Was A Little Bear*
* *Old Maid - Alaska Style (card game)*
.... *and more*

Look at these books by visiting our website **www.alaskachildrensbooks.com**

When Grandma visited Alaska she...

A Children's Book
by
Bernd and Susan Richter

Published by
Saddle Pal Creations, Inc., Wasilla, Alaska

Do you know where Alaska is? If you were in a spaceship high above the earth and you looked out the window, this is what you might see.
Can you find your home on this map? If you can't, Grandma will help you. She will also show you where she and some of your other relatives live. If your home isn't on this map, then you live very, very far away.
If Alaska is so far away, how do you think Grandma got there?

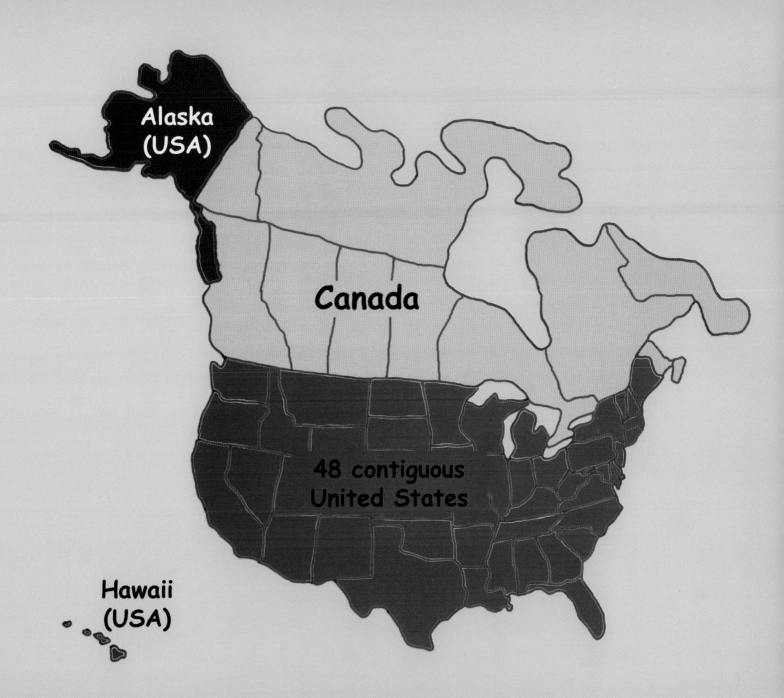

The fastest way for Grandma to get to Alaska is by airplane. Ask Grandma if she flew to Alaska, how long the flight took, and if she enjoyed it. Have you ever flown? If so, did you like it?

In Alaska, the three major cities, Anchorage, Fairbanks and Juneau, are where most of the big airplanes land. Grandma will tell you if she visited these cities and what she did there.

If Grandma didn't arrive in Alaska by airplane, she may have traveled by ship.

Do you know what a cruise ship is? They are huge ships. Cruise ships have space for hundreds or thousands of passengers. Because those ships are on the ocean for many days at a time, they have bedrooms for all the passengers and crew. They also have dining rooms and shops. The biggest cruise ships even have swimming pools!

Have you ever been on a ship or a boat? If so, tell Grandma about your boating adventures.

From the ship, passengers see the coast and the tall mountains of Alaska. Some of these mountains are so high that the snow on them never melts. As the snow gets thicker with each winter, glaciers are formed. Glaciers are like frozen rivers made of snow and ice. Just like rivers, they flow from high elevations to low elevations, only much, much slower. In fact, they move so slowly that one can't tell that they are moving except when pieces of ice break off at the very front of it. When pieces fall off into water they are called icebergs.

What do you think happens to icebergs in the water? Will they float, will they sink to the bottom, or will they melt? Find out when you take your next bath. Ask your mom or dad to put some ice cubes into your bath water. Then watch what happens to the ice.

People on the ships like to watch animals that live in the ocean. Can you name any animals that live in the water?

Have you ever heard of sea otters? In Alaska, everybody loves watching sea otter families because otters are so cute and playful, just like little children. Otters often swim right next to the ships eating crabs and clams. They do that while floating on their backs. Floating is easy for them because they have thick fur that traps air and works just like an air mattress. Grandma will tell you if and where she saw any of those cute sea otters.

Many whales live in the waters off the coast of Alaska. Sometimes whales can be seen swimming at the ocean surface. The tops of their heads show during breathing, and their tails pop up just as they dive again. When they are having lots of fun playing, they sometimes jump all the way out of the water.

Ask Grandma if she saw a whale in Alaska and how big it was. Did you know that some whales can be as long as a huge truck with a trailer?
That's BIG!

Many birds live along the coast. Some of them are the same kinds of birds that live in your backyard. Others live only in faraway places, such as Alaska. One of these is the puffin, shown in this picture. With its yellow and red beak and with its orange legs and feet, it can be seen from far away.

Have you ever seen such a funny looking bird? Of course, they aren't funny if you are a fish! Are there any similar birds where you live? Can you name any birds that live in your backyard?

The ships stop at villages and towns along the coast to let passengers go sightseeing. And there is lots to see and plenty to do!

Just look at this interesting house with totem poles. Do you know where totem poles come from? Totem poles are carved by Native people of Alaska out of very tall trees. The carvings show faces of people and different animals, such as frogs, birds, and fish. These faces and animals tell family stories just like this picture book tells a story.

Can you find any frogs on these totem poles? What else can you find?

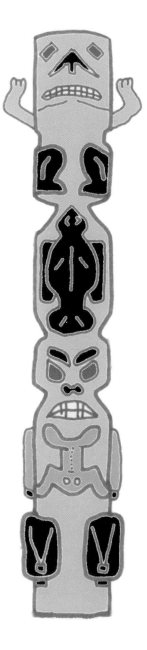

Since Alaska is a very big state, many visitors take a train to see more of the land. The train runs from the coast to the Interior. On the way, passengers can see huge mountain ranges, including Mt. McKinley, North America's highest mountain, and large forests, big rivers, and sometimes even grizzly bears. Have you ever been on a train? If not, would you like to ride on one? Maybe Grandma will take you on a ride someday.

The train stops at Denali National Park where many wild animals live. This park is like a huge zoo but without any fences. All the animals, even the big grizzly bears, can wander around wherever they want to. They find their own food and take care of themselves. Wild animals remain free in their wilderness home in Denali Park.

Can you find in this picture some of the animals that live in the park? Can you show Grandma the bear, the wolf, the caribou, and the moose?
Ask Grandma what animals she saw.

Denali National Park

Did you find the moose? If not, here's one closer up. Have you ever seen a moose before? Are there any moose where you live?

Moose are usually even bigger than horses. Male moose can be recognized easily by their big antlers which grow on their heads each year. Can you think of other animals with antlers? Or how about animals with horns?

What kind of food do you think a moose likes to eat? Often, one can see moose feeding in small ponds or lakes. Could they be eating fish? NO! Moose don't eat fish! They love to eat the juicy grasses that grow on the bottom of lakes. But they also like leaves from alder bushes. And in the winter, when ponds are frozen and leaves have fallen, they eat the tender branches off bushes and trees.

Whoa, what do we have here? Have you ever seen a bear? Not a teddy bear but a REAL bear? One place to see bears is in a zoo. There they are kept in cages or behind big walls because bears can be very dangerous. In Alaska, bears still live in the wild. In the spring, one can see bear moms with their cubs that were born during last winter and now like to play in the meadows after all the snow has melted. Mama bear watches out so that nobody comes too close to her cubs. That's why Grandma stayed far away and hid when she watched the bears and other wild animals. Do you think Grandma was scared when she saw bears in the wild? Would you have been scared?

Where the trains and ships can't go, Grandma can travel by automobile. Some people actually drive their own cars all the way to Alaska, others rent one while there. Many use recreational vehicles, just like this one. Those are great for travel because they have a kitchen, beds, TV, and even a bathroom.

Have you ever been in such a recreational vehicle? Do you think you would rather sleep in one of them or in a tent? How about when it rains?

Ask Grandma if she tried camping while she was in Alaska.

Many people come to Alaska because there are lots of big fish in its rivers. Every summer, hundreds of thousands of fish called salmon swim from the ocean up the rivers to the places where they were born a few years earlier.
This is called a salmon run. When that happens, people rush to the rivers to either watch the run or to catch the fish. Ask Grandma if she saw some red salmon and if she possibly even caught some. Do you eat fish? Salmon taste very good!

Not everybody goes to the rivers for the fish. Instead some go there to search for gold. Do you know what gold is? Can you name or show Grandma something that is made from gold?

Looking for gold is hard work. At the river, this miner first digs holes in the ground with a shovel. He then puts everything he dug up into a gold pan. Finally, he washes the gravel, sand, and mud out of the gold pan into the river. If he is lucky, there will be gold left in the pan after all the hard work. This miner is happy because he found some big gold nuggets. Ask Grandma if she panned for gold and if she was as lucky as this miner.

Can you imagine a place where it doesn't get dark at night?

9 P.M.   Midnight   3 A.M

Well, Alaska is such a place during the summer. It doesn't get dark because the sun goes down very late at night and rises again soon after in the morning. In northernmost Alaska, the sun doesn't set at all for two full months in the middle of the summer! Then children play outside when it's already dark where you live and people go to sleep when it's still light outside. Would you like that? Do you think you could sleep if it wouldn't get dark in your room?

Just the opposite happens in the winter. In northern Alaska in the middle of the winter, the sun never comes up in the morning at all and it stays dark all day. In fact, along the northern coast of Alaska, it is dark for two months in a row! This is a great time to see the northern lights. Do you know what northern lights are? They are bright bands of light, mostly gray, but sometimes pink, red, or green. They swirl around the sky as if someone had turned on a huge multicolored flash-light and pointed it at the dark sky. When the lights are visable starting in late summer, people go outside and watch them just like people watch fireworks at New Year's.

Ask Grandma if she saw the northern lights. Ask her, too, if you can see northern lights where you live.

In the northernmost part of Alaska around the North Pole, it is so cold that the entire ocean is filled with ice and icebergs. This is where Alaska's largest land animal, the polar bear, lives. Because not many other animals live in the frozen North, polar bears have to be good hunters to find their food.

Not many people go to see polar bears in the wild because the bears are very dangerous and because they live so far away. Instead, most people go to a zoo to see polar bears. Have you been to a zoo? If you haven't, maybe Grandma will take you to a zoo one day.

At a time almost as long ago as when the dinosaurs lived, an animal even bigger than the polar bear - the woolly mammoth - made its home in Alaska . The woolly mammoth looked a lot like an elephant except that it had very long fur to protect it from the cold. Today, there are no mammoths left in Alaska, so Grandma couldn't see one in the wild. But maybe one of your ancient relatives saw them a long time ago while visiting Alaska. Can you find the people in this picture who might have been your old relatives?

Once in a while, the bones of mammoths are found by people digging holes in the ground. These bones are then brought to museums for display. Ask Grandma to take you to such a museum one day. There are lots of neat things to do and to see.

After Grandma visited all these great places, it was time for her to go back home. She was really looking forward to seeing her family again, her friends and neighbors, and especially you! Because she loves you, and because she liked Alaska so much, she brought you this pretty picture book as a gift. A few years from now when you are grown up, perhaps you will remember all the pictures Grandma showed you and all the stories she told you.

With much love from:

....

Good-bye, Alaska!

Your Photos Here

Your Travel Log Here

Your Photos Here

Your Travel Log Here